# Forever in the Wind

C.M. Lundervold

BookLeaf Publishing

India | USA | UK

Presentation by *BookLeaf Publishing*

Web: www.bookleafpub.com

E-mail: info@bookleafpub.com

ISBN: 978-93-5744-943-4

First edition 2022

# DEDICATION

To my Dad, for always being my #1 Fan;

and to Mrs. Audrey LaScala, for inspiring me to become a writer all those years ago. Thank you for helping me discover my passion.

# ACKNOWLEDGEMENT

Becoming a writer has been my dream since Kindergarten. I will never forget the love and support from my teacher, who threw a party for the "book" I wrote and shared with the class. It was a lifelong impact, and I adore it.

My dad has supported me all my life. I share my stories with him every so often, and his reaction boosts my confidence every time. He inspired me to pursue my dream to become a writer, and I will never forget his unconditional love and support.

# PREFACE

I took the challenge to provide twenty-one
different poems for the first twenty-one days of
October. With the combination of brand new
poems written just for the occasion and personal
favorites from an earlier time, I successfully
provided twenty-one poems for this very
collection.

I started writing poetry on a less-casual
more-serious level during my senior year of high
school, late 2019. I signed up for a poetry
contest hosted by the SWiC foundation,
Schuylkill Women in Crisis. I won first place
with the poem "Keep Driving," which is
included in this book. I love writing poems, and
this is only the start of my poetry publications.

# It Takes Two

It takes two
To love and be loved.
I am one,
Who is two?

Two is the breeze in the air,
Dazzled with puffs of fluff.
Two is the leaves in the trees,
Rustling with nuts for the heart.

Two is many, not just another
Fellow or man, woman, mind.
Two is everything, for love
Takes much, as much is to give.

Two is lovely, just as one
Is a part of two. It is not
Two ones, but rather one
Plus one means all.

It takes two, except
It is never only
Two. Two means
Everything.
Lovely.

# Heavy Boots

Boots are heavy, heavy boots, heavy boots,
Trudging through carpet, wind slamming doors
     shut.
Mud streaks appear, from heavy boots, heavy
Boots are being untied. Dry mud flakes from
Heavy boots, heavy boots, bang against wood
On the hallway floor. Heavy boots. Mud, mud
On the floor, mud on the floor... Heavy boots
Breaking down wood, make room for muddy
     floor.
Mother is gone. Her wife cries. The baby
Is scared. The boots are heavy. Heavy tears.

# Autumn Reds

The vibrant reds of autumn fall, so free
They are, as summer ends reflect my doubts
Of love's capacity within me. Freeze
This moment, strike the coals, ignite without
The fear of failure. Find myself again.
These bonfires, as red as leaves, caress
My cheeks. They're stained with rivers. Red is
      when
My heart can beat. My heart can beat, and yet
It aches. It craves. It yearns. It wants too much
From lovely boys, who barely reach the bar,
Or lovely girls, with cheeks that rarely blush
From my attempt with words. This red gives
      scars.

The fire cackles, laughs at dreams, my aches
And longings. I will fall, as love red makes.

# Dance

My promised intellect holds no weight, for
Her windows clothed enchant me. I'm in awe
Of her finesse. Am I subpar in lore
Of love? Of her love? I am rich in flaws,
Yet not a soul upon this Earth escapes
The wrath of imperfection. What is it
That makes my love so frail, it always breaks?
Such deep emotions are so strong, yet witt
Of these displays of love I've yet to learn.
This ignorance cause pains, for I've always
Learned best hands-on. Love, true, differs. I
       yearn
To share my virgin lips and meet her gaze.

My ignorance transcends the very chance
To hold her love; at least I'm free to dance.

# She

Where is she?
Who is she?
I thought I knew her,
But whenever I go near,
She is another hill away.

Is she near?
Is she far?
I almost caught her hand,
But after I miss,
She is farther than before.

Is she her?
Is she me?
How can I know her,
See her, hear her, feel her,
If I can't find my shadow?

# Cavern

This cavern is deep,
My sounds come back loud.
I tried to scale the walls,
But with scrapes and bruises,
I fall back down.
I've been trapped before,
Under boulders and cracks,
But I've always lived here.
Why should I leave?

I always see rays of sun
And birds flying overhead.
I have a good view from down here.
Why do I try to escape this home?
It's dark, but I can see light.
It is so much harder to climb
Than to sit back and let
Life go on by.
How did I even get here?

I've not the memory of coming here.
I didn't even notice where I was at first.
How did I get here?
Why can't I get out?
I'm weak, but I'm getting stronger.

It'd be nice to take someone's hand,
But I fear trapping them with me.
I'd rather be trapped alone
Than ruin someone's day.
Perhaps I can only be happy
By stepping on others,
But that is no way to live.

I stare up the cavernous walls
And long to feel the sun
Rather than just feel the heat
Lick at my clothes. Someday,
I will get out.
So long as I keep trying,
I'm sure to get strong enough
To pull myself out one day.
Maybe I'll even be strong enough
To have the courage to
Take someone's hand.

# Moon

The moon mocks me.
It taunts me with its light, unbounded by
Its energy, for it simply mirrors
The shining sun, its light; the moon mocks me:
The way it changes with phases, simply
To start anew again; I envy it.
I envy its power, radiance, light…
I envy its unmatched perseverance,
Its certainty that it will rise again
And fall according to scripted lifetime,
Its innate respect from cultures worldwide.
I could only dream to be heard by
A speck of dust. Plans never seem to work
When I hold the pen; do I have the right?

# Impossible

Why do impossible spirits draw mine?
They taunt me with their presence,
Dancing just out of reach,
Yet my ignorance forbids me from them.
Does ignorance lie?
Does my intellect deceive me?
Am I looking down at the other side of the scale
Or down the stairs of the universal journey?
Are we on the same floor, but across the hall?
At the other end of the building?
What words connect our worlds?
Is it a solid stone bridge
Or a feeble, old radio signal?
Do we coexist only on a shared line of sight?
Is it that my soul's lone cries
Echo within this cavern,
Or is it that our souls long for one another,
Yet neither say a word?
I am a neglected rotisserie chicken
At the perfect temperature,
Yet I sit in the oven with nobody around:
I fear being burnt to a crisp.
I have so much to offer
Yet nobody to share with.
If I don't give gold to those

Other than those who share my heart,
I would have burdened gold shoulders,
Enough to weigh me down and crush bones.
I long to embellish them with
Gold and silver, valuable stones
For invaluable heights,
Though I fear the thought
Of being robbed and dropped.
I'd love to fly,
But I keep linking chains.

# Keep Driving

Endless possibilities, full of life,
Don't deserve to be chained, fueled by strife, or
Barred by fear and apprehension of pain.
Life is blissful when fear is not about.
Others enhance that bliss when all is calm,
Yet some spew devastation brutally
At any sign of happiness or joy.
This is not the way to live, trapped within
The heavy fog of fear, incapable
Of seeing through the torment one is in.
When the high beams of consciousness shine
        through
To no avail, the road will still be there.
Remember: the road will always be there.
The fog light will guide you to better times.

# Gold

Of five golden rings,
All polished and shined,
Four long for the end,
To fall to their demise.
Four have fallen, one by one,
But found and replaced.
Four have lost their posh,
Yet their gold still remained.
Outside eyes adored the glimmer
Of the fitted ring whose
Curvature never changed, yet the
Eyes of the beholder adore all gold
And cherish them for years to come.
The loss of one ring
Matters not to the finger
But to the world of the beholder.
Once gold is lost, it cannot be returned.
Whether pure or impure,
Gold is cherished.
Whether pure or impure,
Gold holds wealth.
Whether pure or impure,
Gold holds memories.
Whether pure or impure,
The loss of one is the loss of many.

Many of which seem small yet hold
Significance so pure,
It cannot be repeated;
Significance so pure,
It cannot be transferred to
Differing mediums.
Once gold is lost, it cannot be returned.
Hold gold preciously, no matter the damage.
The damaged holds irreplicable wealth
As much as the perfect.
Once gold is lost, it cannot be returned.
Once gone, the memory will never retire.
The memory is forever starved.
Once gold is lost, it cannot be returned.
Once altered, it can never be the same.
Accept what is true; love what remains.
Once gold is lost, it cannot be returned.
Once lost, gold cannot be found.
Lost is forever, but memories immortal.
Once gold is lost, it cannot be returned.
One slip may be enough.
Once gold is lost, it cannot be returned.
Keep gold close, for
Once gold is lost, it cannot be returned.

# Ignorance

Maybe it's not ignorance,
But rather pure intelligence
That simply leaves my conscious thought
As I try to release it.

Maybe it's not ignorance,
But genius thoughts that are bestowed
Upon a mind incapable
Of understanding intellect.

Maybe it is ignorance
That I just cannot dominate
No matter how far my reach goes
To try and let it in my soul.

Maybe it is ignorance
That I have simply held so long
That fingers are gripped tight around,
So tight it feels so wrong to let it go.

# Arduous



Whisking winds stir breath,
Raking lungs,
Barbed air gashing pipes.
Fibbing words whiplash minds,
Poor in strength, rich in fatigue.
Arduous,
Too much so to stand.

# Ignite

Need a place to go -
Where is it?
They're everywhere,
Around,
Why can't I move?
No one's stopping me,
Something's stopping me.
My legs are free
But why aren't they moving?

It's right there,
In front of me,
Why haven't I moved?
My blood is warm,
My stomach is full;
Why am I cold and starved?
I have a roof over my head
And a bed to sleep at night,
Why am I drenched and drained?
There are people dying;
There are people starving;
I shouldn't want to be with them,
But I long to sit with them;
I long to starve with them;
I long to talk to them;

I long to laugh with them;
My feeble mind longs
To make their world brighter.
Maybe that's why I'm so cold:
I have a match with nothing to ignite.

# Belong

For all my life he was my knight,
And even now he holds the light
I follow in the darkest night,
And yet the truth holds no delight.

The sword I've always thought he held
Is only pure love he expelled.
Yet acid rain had caused his fall,
The rain upon his tender shell.

Protective towards his kin and I
While desperate for the life's goodbye
While he himself strives to deny
The calming thoughts of his demise.

And yet we all trudge on
For we cannot simply begone
For destiny promised a dawn
Where we belong, where we belong.

# Sand

Laid the pavement over the sand,
Everything falls apart,
Yet scorched sand coats rough stone
With glass smooth, with glass jagged.
Don't dig, you'll get stabbed.
Don't walk atop, you'll fall;
It'll break.
How will you move?

# Hole

So much filling in a gaping hole,
Yet it goes right through the bottom.
Regardless of the quantity,
It is foolish to expect it to fill.
Golden thread hits the bottom;
Everything else is meer child's play.
Yet, innocence is worth just as much.

# Stronger

Over and over and over again,
I found myself in the same place:
Chained,
Restrained,
Bounded.
The walls keep coming back,
Though it's nice how
They seem to be getting thinner;
Maybe I'm just getting stronger.

# Afraid

Are you afraid?
Staring eyes have no lid.
They see you.
Are you afraid?
They are fast.
They follow you,
Regardless of where you go.

# Fraud

It wants to escape me,
My chest, my lungs, my head.
It wants to leave me behind
And everything else gone,
Gone to waste.
It has built so much,
From bridges to temples,
So it would be a shame for it to go.
The bridges are simple yet
Can hold a thousand men,
And the temples are dotted and streaked
With inscriptions untranslatable
By a simple mind. Simple mind.
What defines a simple mind?
What defines a simple kind?
A kind of person, so strong
And full of sense that it needs
No extra drug or treatment
To get through day to day.
If they be simple, I no longer
Wish to be great, for
Being great brings along
Great weights, weights too great
For my weak soul. How come
Such a weak soul bears

So much weight? Is this greatness?
Or is this an illusion masked by
Gifted hubris since the door of the womb?
If it be an illusion, I would not
Be considered great. I would be
Considered a fraud.
I'd much rather be found simple
Than a fraud.

# Possessed

To be possessed is to be free from all
Responsibilities. No freedom means
No worries or remorse, for the appall
Is foolish for all those who lack a screen
Defining all their qualities; for shame.
The individual who has a brain
Will never take a sum without a blame
On someone else who's taken more; the gain
Is too important to ignore, my friend.
Allow His hands on mine, for I will find
A way to use these hands against the bend
Where longing souls are cursed, no longer kind.

This existential dread may leave me dead,
Yet I won't catch an evitable death.

# Hand

People walk atop one another,
Yet there are no steps upon me;
Why is it that I feel crushed?
I need no one to walk beside me,
Yet it would be nice to be able to
Hold someone's hand.

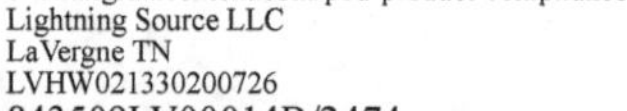